KEEPING PHYSICALLY HEALTHY

Other Books in the LIVING PROUD! Series

Being Transgender

Coming Out and Seeking Support

Confronting Stereotypes

Engaging with Politics

Facing Homophobia

Finding Community

Living with Religion and Faith

Staying Mentally Healthy

Understanding Sexual Orientation and Gender Identity

LIVING PROUD! GROWING UP LGBTQ

KEEPING PHYSICALLY HEALTHY

LAKE PARK HIGH SCHOOL, ROSELLE, IL.

Robert Rodi and Laura Ross

Foreword by Kevin Jennings
Founder, GLSEN (the Gay, Lesbian & Straight
Education Network)

MASON CREST

Mason Crest
450 Parkway Drive, Suite D
Broomall, PA 19008
www.masoncrest.com

Copyright © 2017 by Mason Crest, an imprint of National Highlights, Inc. All rights reserved. No part of this publication may be reproduced or transmitted in any form or by any means, electronic or mechanical, including photocopying, recording, taping, or any information storage and retrieval system, without permission in writing from the publisher.

Printed in the United States of America

First printing
9 8 7 6 5 4 3 2 1

Series ISBN: 978-1-4222-3501-0
Hardcover ISBN: 978-1-4222-3506-5
ebook ISBN: 978-1-4222-8379-0

Cataloging-in-Publication Data is available on file at the Library of Congress.

Developed and Produced by Print Matters Productions, Inc. (www.printmattersinc.com)
Cover and Interior Design by Kris Tobiassen, Matchbook Digital

Picture credits: 10, mediaphotos/iStock; 15, Jason Stitt/Fotalia; 16, Lisa F. Young/Fotalia; 18, 4x6/iStock; 21, Whittle/Splash News/Newscom; 23, imtmphoto/iStock; 24, nico_blue/iStock; 27, Monkey Business/Fotalia; 28, angelhell/iStock; 30, Richard B. Levine/Newscom; 33, ueligiezendanner/iStock; 36, Catherine Lane/iStock; 37, AlexRaths/iStock; 39, camptown/iStock; 42, RalphTV/iStock; 46, Jlcoving/Wikimedia Creative Commons; 47, Wendy Kaveney/Fotalia; 48, syolacan/iStock; 50, princigalli/iStock; 51, Jetrel/iStock; 53, Christopher Futcher/iStock
Front cover: XiXinXing/iStock

KEEPING PHYSICALLY HEALTHY

CONTENTS

Foreword by Kevin Jennings, Founder, GLSEN 8

1. Mind, Body, and Spirit 11
Close-up: The Sad Statistics on LGBT Suicide 12
When Shame Becomes Self-destruction 13
Partners on the Journey 15

2. Body Concept 19
Men and Body Concept 19
The Emotional Weight of Body Fat 21
Close-up: The Causes and Effects of Eating Disorders 25
Women and Body Concept 25
Using Food to Bury Sexuality 27

3. Self-Respect and Sexual Health 31
AIDS and the LGBT Rights Movement 33
Close-up: AIDS Doesn't Discriminate 34
Other Sexually Transmitted Diseases 34
Unsafe Sex 35
Close-up: How to Practice Safer Sex 36
Pregnancy: The Other Risk 38
Do It for Yourself! 40

4. Substance Abuse 43
Gays and Crystal Meth 44
Drugs and Risky Behaviors 46

Lesbians and Alcohol Abuse 49
Tobacco Use 49
Finding Options 51
Close-up: Recovery and Rehabilitation Resources 52

Series Glossary 56

Further Resources 62

Index 64

KEY ICONS TO LOOK FOR

Text-Dependent Questions: These questions send the reader back to the text for more careful attention to the evidence presented there.

Words to Understand: These words with their easy-to-understand definitions will increase the reader's understanding of the text while building vocabulary skills.

Series Glossary of Key Terms: This back-of-the-book glossary contains terminology used throughout this series. Words found here increase the reader's ability to read and comprehend higher-level books and articles in this field.

Research Projects: Readers are pointed toward areas of further inquiry connected to each chapter. Suggestions are provided for projects that encourage deeper research and analysis.

Sidebars: This boxed material within the main text allows readers to build knowledge, gain insights, explore possibilities, and broaden their perspectives by weaving together additional information to provide realistic and holistic perspectives.

FOREWORD

I loved libraries as a kid.

Every Saturday my mom and I would drive from the trailer where we lived on an unpaved road in the unincorporated town of Lewisville, North Carolina, and make the long drive to the "big city" of Winston-Salem to go to the downtown public library, where I would spend joyous hours perusing the books on the shelves. I'd end up lugging home as many books as my arms could carry and generally would devour them over the next seven days, all the while eagerly anticipating next week's trip. The library opened up all kinds of worlds to me—all kinds of worlds, except a gay one.

Oh, I found some "gay" books, even in the dark days of the 1970s. I'm not sure how I did, but I found my way to authors like Tennessee Williams, Yukio Mishima, and Gore Vidal. While these great artists created masterpieces of literature that affirmed that there were indeed other gay people in the universe, their portrayals of often-doomed gay men hardly made me feel hopeful about my future. It was better than nothing, but not much better. I felt so lonely and isolated I attempted to take my own life my junior year of high school.

In the 35 years since I graduated from high school in 1981, much has changed. Gay–straight alliances (an idea my students and I pioneered at Concord Academy in 1988) are now widespread in American schools. Out LGBT (lesbian, gay, bisexual, and transgender) celebrities and programs with LGBT themes are commonplace on the airwaves. Oregon has a proud bisexual governor, multiple members of Congress are out as lesbian, gay, or bisexual, and the White House was bathed in rainbow colors the day marriage equality became the law of the land in 2015. It gets better, indeed.

So why do we need the Living Proud! series?

- Because GLSEN (the Gay, Lesbian & Straight Education Network) reports that over two-thirds of LGBT students routinely hear anti-LGBT language at school.

- Because GLSEN reports that over 60% of LGBT students do not feel safe at school.
- Because the CDC (the Centers for Disease Control and Prevention, a U.S. government agency) reports that lesbian and gay students are four times more likely to attempt suicide than heterosexual students

In my current role as the executive director of the Arcus Foundation (the world's largest financial supporter of LGBT rights), I work in dozens of countries and see how far there still is to go. In over 70 countries same-sex relations are crimes under existing laws: in 8, they are a crime punishable by the death penalty. It's better, but it's not all better—especially in our libraries, where there remains a need for books that address LGBT issues that are appropriate for young people, books that will erase both the sense of isolation so many young LGBT people still feel as well as the ignorance so many non-LGBT young people have, ignorance that leads to the hate and violence that still plagues our community, both at home and abroad.

The Living Proud! series will change that and will save lives. By providing accurate, age-appropriate information to young people of all sexual orientations and gender identities, the Living Proud! series will help young people understand the complexities of the LGBT experience. Young LGBT people will see themselves in its pages, and that reflection will help them see a future full of hope and promise. I wish Living Proud! had been on the shelves of the Winston-Salem/Forsyth County Public Library back in the seventies. It would have changed my life. I'm confident that it will have as big an impact on its readers today as it would have had on me back then. And I commend it to readers of any age.

Kevin Jennings
Founder, GLSEN (the Gay, Lesbian & Straight Education Network)
Executive Director, Arcus Foundation

GLSEN is the leading national education organization focused on ensuring safe and affirming schools for all students. GLSEN seeks to develop school climates where difference is valued for the positive contribution it makes to creating a more vibrant and diverse community.
www.glsen.org

1
MIND, BODY, AND SPIRIT

WORDS TO UNDERSTAND

Discrimination: When someone is treated differently because of his or her race, sexual identity, religion, or some other factor.
LGBT: An acronym or abbreviation for lesbian, gay, bisexual, and transgender. Sometimes a "Q" is added (LGBTQ) to stand for "questioning" or "queer."
Peers: People who are the same age as you, or, more generally, just like you in some other way.
Internalized: Taken inside of one's self; for example, when a person believes the negative opinions other people have of him, he has *internalized* their point of view and made it his own.

Kara Blake is a healthy, vibrant, and proud woman. She's passionate about fighting for LGBT rights, and she's always eager to get involved and assist young people through the complicated process of coming out.

But that wasn't always the case.

"If you'd known me a few years ago, you wouldn't believe it was the same person," she says. "Pretty much anything there was to do to ruin my body, I did it. And I did it a lot. I could say it was because I was unhappy about being gay, but it wasn't that simple. I *thought* I was unhappy being gay, but really I was just sad because I couldn't be me, the real me. And that kind of sadness hits you everywhere, inside and out."

When she was coming out in high school, Kara faced struggles that many young LGBT people experience. To help make herself feel better, or just to numb the pain, she began using drugs with her friends.

Feelings of shame and self-loathing are common in young LGBT people, especially when they encounter rejection by friends, family, schools, churches, and other influential people in their lives. LGBT teens are at a significantly higher risk for mental health problems, such as depression, which in turn can lead to substance abuse and even attempts at suicide.

"[These young people] face **discrimination**, oppression, and low self-esteem," says Julie A. Bock, director of an **LGBT** youth center in Wisconsin. "They also take more risks."

 CLOSE-UP: THE SAD STATISTICS ON LGBT SUICIDE

LGBT youth are four times more likely to attempt suicide than are their heterosexual peers. Suicide attempts by LGBT youth are four to six times more likely to result in injury, poisoning, or overdose that requires treatment from a doctor or nurse, compared to those of their straight peers. LGBT youth who come from highly rejecting families are 8.4 times as likely to have attempted suicide as those who reported no or low levels of family rejection. (Source: The Trevor Project)

MIND, BODY, AND SPIRIT   13

When Shame Becomes Self-destruction

Bock's organization helped a young man named Darien Winston, who had left home when he was eighteen. After realizing he was gay four years earlier, he twice tried to kill himself, believing he was doomed to go to hell because he was gay.

"There are so many things in the world that are painful—this shouldn't be one of them," says out country singer Chely Wright. "This shouldn't be a reason a kid goes into his basement and puts a gun in his mouth. This shouldn't be a reason a forty-five-year-old man takes a bottle of pills." Of course, not all LGBT people resort to such drastic measures when dealing with the challenges of their sexual orientation.

And there are many other health issues that affect LGBT people differently from their heterosexual **peers**. Even something as simple as going for a medical check-up can be frightening for LGBT people. As a result, they are less likely to maintain this crucial aspect of a healthy lifestyle. Many fear coming out to their doctors in case they face judgment or prejudice from physicians who don't typically treat LGBT patients.

"My mom always took me to the doctor when I was in school," says Kara. "So she would be sitting right there, and the doctor would ask me questions about sexual activities and things like that. Did I use drugs? What was I supposed to say? I couldn't tell the truth because my mom would have gone crazy. So I lied."

Kara found herself lying about many things when faced with issues related to her sexual orientation. She couldn't be honest about who she was to her family or her friends, so being gay started to feel like a shameful secret. She began to hate herself for being gay.

That feeling is known as **internalized** homophobia. It occurs when external pressures—from friends, family, or society in general—send such strong homophobic messages that LGBT people believe there is something wrong with them.

"I wished, each and every day, that I wasn't gay," says Kara. "If there was a pill that could have made me straight, I would have taken it, without a doubt. I wanted to just be 'normal.' That's why I don't understand people who think being gay is a choice. I would never have chosen to feel that way. Never."

Those negative emotions and feelings of self-hatred took a physical toll on Kara. For years, she struggled with an eating disorder, abused drugs and alcohol, and engaged in risky sexual behavior that could have had severe consequences.

It wasn't until she found a supportive and welcoming group of friends in the LGBT community that she began to accept and love herself. Those feelings of anger and self-hatred no longer exist for her.

"Now I'd say, 'A straight pill? No thanks!'" she says with a smile. "I love who I am. I love my life. I wouldn't want to change any of it.

"Taking care of yourself and respecting yourself make all the difference. I didn't respect myself enough to stand up for myself. I let other people dictate to me how I was supposed to be and act. I let them beat me up, and I didn't even raise a hand to defend myself. So now, I just try to help kids see that it really does get better. It's not always going to be like that. But they have to care enough about themselves to take care of their minds and bodies."

MIND, BODY, AND SPIRIT   15

LGBT teens face many challenges to their self-esteem. If something as basic as your sexual or gender identity is not accepted by your family, friends, and community, it can be very hard to feel good about yourself.

Partners on the Journey

Today, more than ever before, advocacy organizations help LGBT people find the resources and support they need. At community centers like the one Bock leads, the staff is trained to deal with even the most complicated and seemingly hopeless situations. These professionals can also help young people deal with day-to-day challenges and questions.

"We work closely with young people to resolve whatever is going on in their lives. There is nothing that's forbidden," Bock says. "You want to talk about safe sex, that's fine. We go there. Whatever the crisis is, we help them resolve it."

LGBT centers offer discussion groups, social events, and classes on health and fitness. Most of them provide condoms and information about safer sex. Some even offer rapid HIV testing that provides results in 20 minutes, making it easier for people to get accurate results quickly.

For those who don't have such a center in their area—or are afraid to visit one—there are hundreds of resources online. The National Gay and Lesbian Task Force offers numerous resources for LGBT youth. The Trevor Project provides help for individuals considering suicide, including a 24-hour telephone help line. The GLBT National Help Center has peer-supported online chat, as well as toll-free peer-counseling support

LGBT organizations help young people deal with day-to-day challenges and questions as well as crisis situations.

MIND, BODY, AND SPIRIT

lines. The Gay and Lesbian Medical Association's website helps LGBT people find health care providers who are LGBT friendly and familiar with the specific needs of the LGBT community.

"It's so important to take care of yourself—your mind, body, and spirit," says Kara. "It's all connected. Someone can look perfect on the outside but be a mess on the inside. And what good is that? That's never going to make you happy. You have to find your peace in life. That's what makes you feel good. When you are at peace with yourself and who you are, everything else just falls into place."

TEXT-DEPENDENT QUESTIONS

- What are some ways that internalized homophobia becomes self-destructive?
- How do health issues affect LGBT people differently from straight people?
- What makes advocacy organizations so valuable to LGBT teens with self-esteem issues?

RESEARCH PROJECTS

- Make a list of things you think might help boost someone's self-esteem.
- Make a list of things you might say to someone who you thought was suicidal or self-destructive.
- Visit the Trevor Project's website, and check out what they do and how they do it.

Masculinity comes in all shapes and sizes and is not defined by the stereotypical image of big muscles and six-pack abs.

2
BODY CONCEPT

WORDS TO UNDERSTAND

Effeminate: A word used to refer to men who have stereotypically feminine qualities.
Emasculated: Having had one's masculinity or manhood taken away.
Subculture: A smaller group of people with similar interests and lifestyles within a larger group.

Flipping through the pages of magazines, you're likely to find certain kinds of images: beautiful skinny women and ruggedly handsome men with fashionable clothes and perfectly toned bodies—all revealing charming smiles and sparkling white teeth. These images may be attractive, but they are also potentially harmful.

Men and Body Concept

Youth, beauty, and muscles... these are a few of the things that gay men such as Ed Wesley may enjoy looking at but don't necessarily relate to personally.

"We don't really have gay role models who are just ordinary-looking guys," he says. "It's all six-pack abs and beautiful young faces. The first 'big guy' gay man I'd ever seen was on *Modern Family*."

He was referring to the television comedy that premiered in 2009 and features a gay couple, Mitchell and Cameron. Mitchell is slender, but Cameron is bigger and bulkier—just like Ed.

When Ed was first venturing out of the closet, decades before *Modern Family*, he recognized that he didn't fit the traditional image of a gay man, which made him feel like even more of an outsider. To fit into his own community, he felt pressure to conform to an image. Gay bars and clubs in West Hollywood seemed like the best places for him to meet people, but his husky frame, pale skin, and bald head didn't fit the standard set by the suntanned men with chiseled muscles that he encountered there.

Although Ed eventually learned to be comfortable with himself and his body, some gay men don't. About 40 percent of men with eating disorders identify as gay or bisexual. Studies show this may be a reaction to something called "minority stress," defined as the perceived need to meet mainstream standards of masculinity. For LGBT people, this can be "strike two," when combined with the fear and pressure that can accompany coming out in the first place.

Some gay men feel that they will be safer from homophobic people if they look like typical straight men. "A lot of men who were sort of sissy boys . . . at school, and were **effeminate**, did feel themselves **emasculated**," says David Watkins, author of the novel *Fat Land: Thin Is In. Insides Are Out*. "So, trying to attain a definitive male body is trying to regain some of that maleness for themselves. It's trying to reclaim their masculinity because they lost it so early on. And they

Stereotypical images of masculinity in media and advertising can be confusing for young gay and bisexual men who are trying to find themselves and their sexual identity.

kind of want it back, so they go for that male ideal of the big muscles and the six-pack and the strong chest and the flat stomach."

The Emotional Weight of Body Fat

David is one of seven gay men who participated in *Do I Look Fat?*, a 2005 documentary about eating disorders and body image in the gay community. The film explores "self-esteem disorder" and the lack of support for young gay people that can lead to feelings of sadness, depression, and loneliness.

Stu, another subject of the film, recalls the effect his childhood had on his relationship with food. When he was in junior high school, he felt isolated and alone. "I remember being called a 'fag' even though I didn't know what it was," he says. "I remember walking to and from school. Most kids took the school bus, and I think, because I wanted to be by myself, I walked. And I remember stopping at the bakery and getting a chocolate éclair. Even then . . . food was my friend and it was very comforting to me."

David points out that body image issues take root when young gay people are struggling to come to terms with both their sexual orientation and how they fit in with their peers.

"Guys who had extra weight on, guys who were walking around with a few more pounds, guys who had breasts or bellies—this was a female thing to have, a fuller figure," he says. "I was inactive, and boys at school were always playing sports and always running around. So you do, in some ways, get emasculated as a fat kid. You don't necessarily really connect as a boy or a man."

That sense of not being a "real man" is more complicated for young gay men than straight ones because they are subject to the societal and cultural message that being gay is weird or strange. And when the pressure of these judgments becomes too intense, it can have damaging results.

"It's this [idea that] fat equals weak, equals female. Thin equals strong, equals male," David says. "And when you're gay, gay equals weak, equals female. So you do anything to be gay equals strong, equals man. And that means exercising to the point of extreme . . . or just not eating, full stop. Anything to be thin. Anything to be a man."

BODY CONCEPT   23

If a gay man is not tall, thin, and muscular, he may feel as though he's less masculine. Nothing could be further from the truth. Masculinity takes all shapes and sizes.

Some gay teens may feel as though the only way to be masculine is to have a muscular physique.

For some gay men, this can mean using steroids to enhance their muscles, working out at the gym obsessively, using drugs to lose weight and be thin, or developing an **eating disorder**. Each of these behaviors can have serious side effects that cause severe and lasting damage. Steroid use can cause high blood pressure and stunted growth in adolescents. Excessive exercise can cause damage to joints and ligaments, and eating disorders can cause malnutrition, dehydration, and muscle and tissue damage.

CLOSE-UP: THE CAUSES AND EFFECTS OF EATING DISORDERS

Eating disorders are psychiatric disorders characterized by abnormal eating habits that may involve either eating too much or too little, to the point that the level of food intake is dangerous to the individual's physical and emotional health. Binge-eating disorder, bulimia nervosa (eating followed by induced vomiting), and anorexia nervosa (self-starvation) are the most common eating disorders in the United States. The causes of these are complex and poorly understood, though it is clear that they are often associated with other conditions and social situations. For example, one study found that girls with ADHD are many times more likely to develop certain eating disorders, and another found that women raised in foster care are also many times more likely to develop bulimia nervosa. It is generally thought that peer pressure and pressure from the idealized body types portrayed in the media are also significant factors.

In the United States, 5 to 10 million women and about 1 million men suffer from an eating disorder. But nearly 42 percent of the men identify as gay or bisexual. In fact, gay men are more than three times more likely to suffer an eating disorder than heterosexuals; and 15 percent of gay or bi men have struggled throughout their lives with binge eating, anorexia, or bulimia.

While proper treatment can be effective for many types of eating disorders, the consequences of eating disorders can be severe, including death.

Women and Body Concept

Though women in the LGBT community can also struggle with their body image and self-esteem, the issues are slightly different. Women in general, gay or straight, face pressure to fit into cultural stereotypes of how a female should appear. Supermodels with perfectly proportioned bodies are a difficult standard to live up to!

But studies have found that gay women are also influenced by a lesbian **subculture**, which in many ways rejects traditional roles for women. Lesbian teens trying to sort through their personal identity can then become very confused and conflicted about what they are expected to look like and be.

"When I was in high school, there were gay girls who were really athletic and on the soccer team or the softball team, and that wasn't me," says Kara Blake, who first recognized she was gay while in middle school. "I was a cheerleader. I didn't want to be butch or look like a boy. And because of that, I didn't fit in with the people who were gay. So I tried even harder to fit in with my friends, but it was so difficult because I knew I wasn't like them. They wanted to look sexy and have boyfriends, and I just didn't. It was exhausting to try to live up to that."

Throughout high school, Kara battled depression, and eventually turned to drugs and alcohol to make herself feel better. She was so unhappy that she also began overeating. Her binge eating and alcohol consumption resulted in a weight gain of 30 pounds—an unhealthy amount for her once lean and fit frame.

"Then I didn't fit in anywhere," she says. "I think I did it because I didn't want the boys to be interested in me. Because then if they didn't want me, it wasn't because I was gay. It was *them*. So I didn't have to tell my friends that I wasn't with a boy because I was a lesbian. It was just because I was fat."

BODY CONCEPT 27

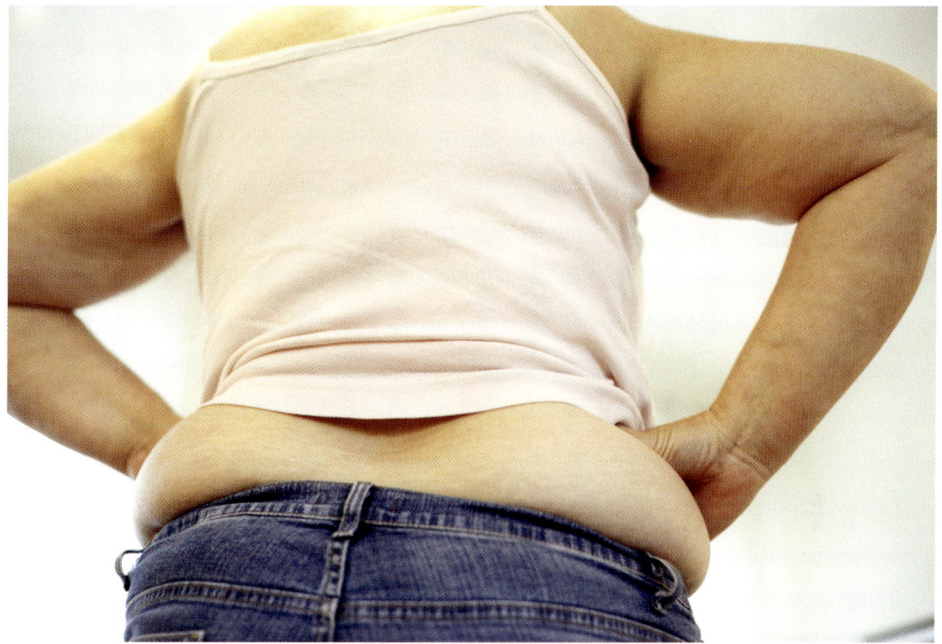

For a lesbian teenager struggling with her sexual orientation, gaining weight may be an attempt to create a barrier against heterosexual relationships.

Using Food to Bury Sexuality

Jai, who was also featured in the documentary *Do I Look Fat?*, had a similar perspective when he was struggling with his identity. He believed he could avoid issues of sexuality by making himself undesirable to other people.

"Part of the theory is that . . . if you're unsure of where you are, or if you're just not comfortable with it, using the eating disorder is an incredibly effective way to feel nonsexual," he says. "And part of me probably knew this, making myself seem less appealing, looking sick, looking sad."

Jai was treated for his eating disorder and drug addiction. Part of the recovery process was about establishing a healthy relationship with his body and himself. Experts recommend that anyone struggling with body image

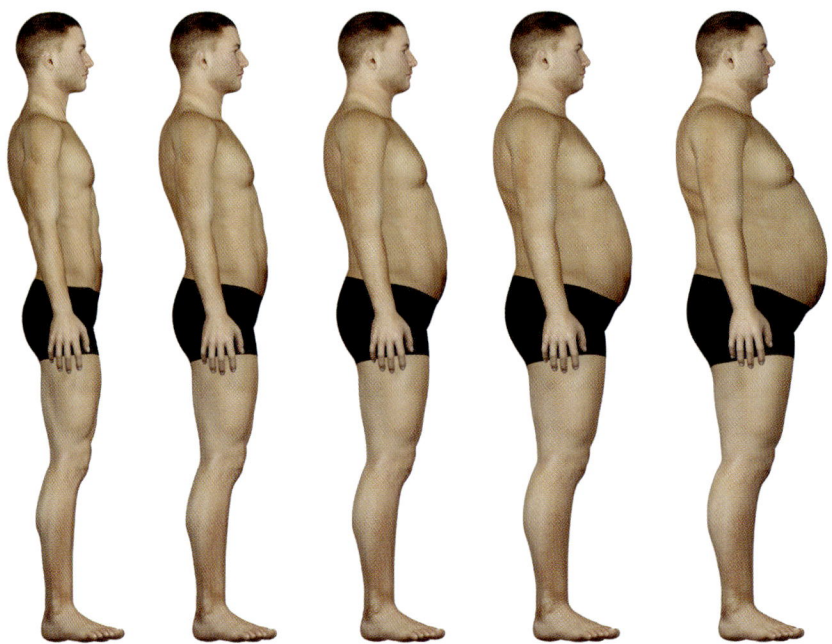

Both gaining unhealthy amounts of weight and losing unhealthy amounts of weight can be ways of avoiding your own sexuality.

issues or eating disorders should discuss the problem with a professional, a trusted friend, or a support group. There are also rehabilitation centers to assist individuals with eating disorders, including Rogers Memorial Hospital in Wisconsin, which has a residential treatment facility specifically for men.

But the situation doesn't have to be quite so critical for people to take action. In fact, everyone benefits from being aware of their physical health and making sure to find a routine that works. Ed, for example, works hard to eat right and remain active. He has also found social groups and activities where he is surrounded by people who look more like him. And he's never been happier.

Getting regular exercise and eating healthy foods are necessities for all people, gay or straight. Simple exercises, such as walking or running, provide opportunities to burn off calories—along with frustration and anger. Being in good physical condition helps improve an individual's overall body image and self-confidence. It increases self-esteem and personal satisfaction with life.

"I like looking good and feeling good, so that's why I go to the gym," says Jim Mansell, who is in a committed relationship and works out at least five times a week. "People think gay men go to the gym just to meet other guys or something. For some people, that's true. But it also makes you feel good about yourself. When I don't exercise or when I eat too much and just lay on the couch all day, I don't like the way I feel about myself. But when I exercise and keep myself healthy, I feel good about me. And that's most important to me."

TEXT-DEPENDENT QUESTIONS

- Why are body issues often more troubling for LGBT teens than for straight ones?
- How can an obsession with obtaining physical perfection actually be physically harmful?
- How does adding body weight help some people mask other serious issues?

RESEARCH PROJECTS

- Make a list of reasons why a perfect-looking body isn't necessarily a healthy body.
- Make a list of things you might say to someone who suffers from an eating disorder.
- Examine how much your self-esteem depends on your physical appearance; ask yourself whether it's too much.

If you are sexually active, you owe it to yourself and your partners to know your HIV status.

3
SELF-RESPECT AND SEXUAL HEALTH

 WORDS TO UNDERSTAND

Epidemic: A widespread outbreak of disease.
Taboo: Something that is forbidden.
Harassment: Being teased, bullied, or physically threatened on an ongoing basis.
Stigma: A mark of shame.

If you ask someone to name a health issue affecting the LGBT community, you're probably going to get the same answer, over and over: AIDS, or acquired immune deficiency syndrome.

Pride festivals are covered with posters promoting safer sex. Magazines advertise the latest drug treatment therapies. Mobile units park outside gay clubs to offer testing for HIV, the human immunodeficiency virus that causes AIDS.

"It's hard not to think of it as a gay disease," says Rob Kelly. "I don't know any straight people who have it. I mean, I know they do, but in my world, all I see or hear about is gay men. Practically every movie or TV show with gay characters has some mention of HIV. Straight people don't talk about it the way we do."

Like many other young people who didn't experience the AIDS **epidemic** and ensuing panic in the 1980s, he didn't consider HIV to be that much of a threat. People now live with HIV for decades without ever getting sick, and the illness isn't the death sentence it once was. As a result, people aren't as cautious as they once were. That was true for Rob, who didn't recognize the importance of regular testing and safer sex until he tested positive for HIV when he was twenty-one. Worse, the virus had progressed so far in his system that it had already become AIDS by the time he even knew he was infected. The virus had attacked his system so severely that his T cells—the white blood cells that help the body fight infection—were almost gone.

The fact is, people who engage in risky sexual behaviors, no matter what their sexual orientation, are putting themselves at risk of contracting HIV. The disease has nothing to do with personal identity. It's about bodily fluids. Whenever bodily fluids are exchanged—whether through sexual intercourse between heterosexual partners or same-sex partners, or through sharing needles for drugs—HIV can be transmitted.

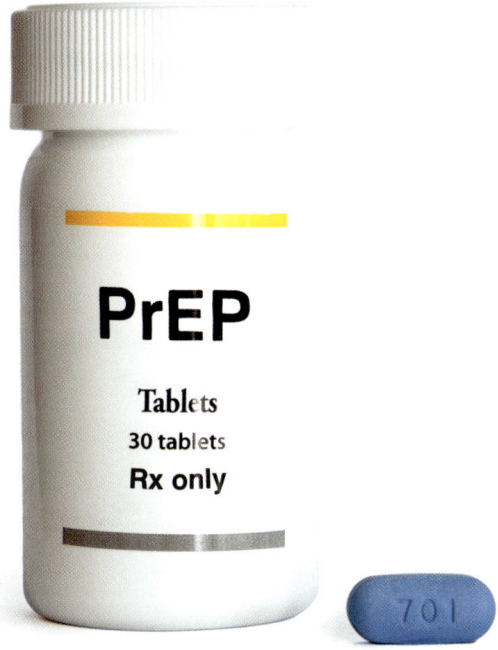

PrEP (pre-exposure prophylaxis) is a relatively new drug combination that when taken daily can reduce the risk of HIV infection through sex by more than 90 percent. PrEP does not protect against other sexually transmitted diseases; condoms do.

AIDS and the LGBT Rights Movement

The history of HIV and AIDS closely mirrors the growth of the LGBT rights movement. When public action to stop the illness was slow to come in the 1980s, many attributed this to the fact that the disease was mostly appearing in the gay community. In fact, it was initially called GRID—gay-related immune deficiency. But the public slowly became aware of the universal nature of the illness when people outside the gay community became infected. Ryan White, a hemophiliac who was infected with HIV at thirteen from a blood transfusion, became nationally recognized when he was expelled from school because of his illness in 1984.

While HIV is an undeniable threat to gay men, it's also a significant risk for anyone who engages in sex without a condom, whether gay or straight. In 2004, 4,883 American youth between the ages of thirteen and twenty-four were infected with HIV, and 232 young people with AIDS died.

 CLOSE-UP: AIDS DOESN'T DISCRIMINATE

A common misconception is that AIDS afflicts only certain groups of people—for instance, the sexually promiscuous, or drug users, or people who live at the poverty level. In fact, HIV is a very democratic virus; it has affected men and women, prostitutes and virgins, meth addicts and movie stars, as well as atheists and believers of every race and on every continent. It's a mistake—and a potentially deadly one—to believe yourself to be immune from it. The only way to keep from contracting AIDS is to avoid the body fluids of those who do have it. Some people—such as infants born to HIV-positive mothers, or hospital patients who receive tainted blood in a transfusion (increasingly a rarity)—are not in a position to safeguard themselves. However, sexually active people are; they can practice safer sex.

Other Sexually Transmitted Diseases

AIDS isn't the only health issue sexual people need to take precautions against. Sexually transmitted diseases (STDs), also known as sexually transmitted infections (STIs) or venereal diseases (VDs), are illness passed from person to person through sexual activity, including vaginal intercourse, oral sex, and anal sex. While in the past, these illnesses have mostly been referred to as STDs or VDs, in recent years, the medical community has begun to prefer the term STIs because it has a broader meaning: A person may be infected, and may potentially infect others, without showing signs of disease. Some STIs can also be transmitted via the use of IV drug needles, as well as through childbirth or breastfeeding. Sexually transmitted infections have been well known for hundreds of years.

A CDC study showed that 47 percent of high school students are sexually active, often before they receive proper education on STDs such as HIV, chlamydia, herpes, and gonorrhea. What many people don't realize is that the most effective way to prevent transmission of these diseases is the simplest: Practice safer sex.

Unsafe Sex

Unfortunately, some people who have unprotected sex remain ignorant of these simple precautions because to engage in a conversation about sex might mean revealing their habits and preferences.

"It is a very **taboo** subject among parents, teachers, everybody. We're hoping by opening up a more honest discussion that teenagers will reduce their amount of sexual activity or use contraception," says Julia Bair, a public health educator. "This is an issue that is so huge, but it tends to get swept under the carpet because people don't want to talk about it."

36 KEEPING PHYSICALLY HEALTHY

 CLOSE-UP: HOW TO PRACTICE SAFER SEX

It's actually very easy to reduce the risk of getting a sexually transmitted disease. Because avoiding the exchange of body fluids is key, wearing a condom is the most effective course of action. Using condoms makes vaginal or anal intercourse safer, and using a condom or similar barrier called a dental dam makes oral sex safer. An even safer practice is to engage in sex play without actual genital-to-genital, or genital–anal, or genital–oral sex. The possibilities are as varied as your imagination.

Safer sex means using a condom for oral sex and vaginal or anal intercourse.

It's not easy to talk about sex in general. And LGBT teens who aren't able to discuss their sexuality with their parents are even more unlikely to take the measures necessary to protect themselves from STDs. The CDC encourages all teens to protect themselves by using condoms, as well as limiting their number of sexual partners or not engaging in sexual activity at all. Teenagers who *are* sexually active need to be open and honest with their doctors so they can be tested for possible infections and receive important information about sexual health.

LGBT teenagers need to find a doctor with whom they feel comfortable discussing their sex life so that they can be tested and treated for possible infections and receive important information about sexual health.

"Discussions around sexual health are never easy or comfortable," says Dr. Marybeth McCall, chief medical officer for Excellus BlueCross BlueShield. "Until we start increasing awareness around the importance of regular screenings for at-risk individuals, many undiagnosed infected individuals will put their health at risk by going untreated—and will threaten the health of others by unknowingly spreading their infection."

Pregnancy: The Other Risk

The other primary risk of unprotected sex is pregnancy. In 2013, 61,800 teenagers in the United States became pregnant. Surprisingly, a significant number of them identified as lesbian or bisexual.

While this may sound confusing, the reason is not difficult to understand. Many gay teens say they've engaged in heterosexual sex so their classmates won't suspect they are gay. Similarly, the study found that a high percentage of gay and bisexual teen males were also involved with pregnancies.

"Those who experience **harassment** and discrimination may choose pregnancy involvement as a way to deny their orientation, to prevent further enacted **stigma**," a study reports.

As a high school student, Kara Blake was terrified that her friends and family would find out she was gay. So to hide it, she had sex with several different boys. She even hoped that if she did it enough, she might be able to force herself to be straight.

But she didn't have any romantic feelings for the boys she was with, and she knew they didn't care about her. Each time, the encounters made her feel worse about herself, which made her increasingly depressed.

SELF-RESPECT AND SEXUAL HEALTH 39

Pregnancy brings with it an entirely new set of responsibilities and health issues, and yet some LGBT teens would rather risk pregnancy than reveal their sexual orientation or gender identity.

"It was so degrading, and it made me feel cheap and used," she says. "After a while, I didn't even care what happened anymore. I never got pregnant, but I could have, because I wasn't always safe. It didn't feel real to me, so I didn't think it mattered if I used a condom. But a lot of things could have happened to me because of that."

Do It for Yourself!

Safer sex may seem like a set of needless rules created by adults to control adolescents. But the reality is this: Safer sex isn't something you do for your parents. It's not something you do for your church or religious leader. You don't do it to please your teachers or your counselors. You do it for yourself.

Sexual health and self-respect go hand-in-hand. All the education, knowledge, and awareness in the world won't mean anything if people don't respect themselves enough to take precautions that will protect them. And this includes selecting appropriate sexual partners.

"To keep your body safe, you have to have pride, no matter if you're gay or straight," says Rob Kelly. "It's the pride of knowing that you're worth taking care of and you're worth protecting. It's not about what other people want or what they say or what they do. It's about you, because the choices you make in one moment can affect your life forever."

TEXT-DEPENDENT QUESTIONS

- Who is at risk for AIDS?
- How does AIDS spread?
- What are some other sexually transmitted diseases?

 RESEARCH PROJECTS

- Read about the early days of the AIDS crisis and its impact on LGBT rights—either online or in books such as *The Band Played On* by Randy Shilts.
- If you don't already have one, find a doctor you feel comfortable talking to about your sexuality and sexual experiences.
- Make a list of safer sex practices that you might enjoy, and make them the basis of your own sexual encounters if and when you are sexually active.

4
SUBSTANCE ABUSE

 WORDS TO UNDERSTAND

Activists: People committed to social change through political and personal action.
Inhibitions: Feelings of guilt and shame that keep us from doing things we might otherwise want to do.

When Simon Fanshawe first came out, he was active in political movements to gain equal rights for LGBT people. His pride in himself and his community was evident in his lifestyle and attitude, so it surprised some people when he produced a documentary titled *The Trouble with Gay Men*.

"We've fought discrimination and prejudice, only to wreck ourselves with drugs," he says.

The film explores frightening trends of substance abuse within the LGBT community, highlighting an issue that **activists** around the world have been working tirelessly to resolve. Studies show that LGBT people are more likely to abuse drugs, alcohol, and tobacco than is the general population.

The National Association of Lesbian and Gay Addiction Professionals notes that LGBT people use drugs and alcohol for many of the same reasons other people do: as a way of coping with stress, depression, or pressure. But these factors are heightened in the LGBT community, where people often face homophobia and rejection by family and friends.

These tensions can be especially difficult for young people. A 1995 study identified substance-abuse risk factors among teens and adolescents, including

- Feelings of being worthless or "bad"
- No support from peers and adults
- Pressure to fit in
- No access to role models
- Few opportunities to socialize with LGBT people outside of bars
- Fear of contracting HIV

No wonder substance abuse is so common among LGBT people!

Gays and Crystal Meth

Crystal methamphetamine, usually referred to simply as "crystal meth," became prevalent in the gay community as a drug used at parties because it lowers **inhibitions** and puts people at ease.

Matt began using crystal meth when he was sixteen. At the time, he knew he was gay. He had tried to tell his parents, but they made it clear that he would not be welcome at home if he lived what they called a "gay lifestyle." In his small town, his religious neighbors were openly homophobic, blaming gay people for drugs and AIDS.

"Whenever there would be stories in the paper or on the news about gay people, it always had something to do with drugs," he says. "My parents would just shake their heads and say, 'It figures.'"

He didn't find support at his school, either. He watched as an older male student came out and caused a panic in the school. Other students bullied him relentlessly, and parents wouldn't allow their sons to be in his gym class. A teacher even told Matt that the boy would get AIDS and die because he was gay.

"They were the people you trust, so I believed them," Matt says. "It didn't even occur to me to doubt them, or to think that maybe they didn't know what they were talking about. I knew I would never, ever tell. I couldn't. I just wanted to get out of there."

He began sneaking out of the house and going to gay bars and clubs. Ashamed of what he was doing and what the consequences might be, he began using crystal meth and other club drugs.

"It made me feel like nothing mattered," he says. "I didn't have to care about anything. I wasn't scared of anything. I was just so out of it, anything could have happened to me."

Crystal meth creates feelings of pleasure in the brain. While this doesn't sound like a bad thing, the drug actually changes how the brain functions, and some of these changes continue after the drug use stops. Long-term users of crystal meth are often unable to produce certain brain chemicals naturally, and so become completely addicted to the drug. Crystal meth also significantly impairs brain function during use.

Crystal meth and other club drugs are particularly tempting to LGBT youth because they lower inhibitions and make you more comfortable with your sexual attraction without having to deal with the more difficult issues involved in figuring out who you are.

Drugs and Risky Behaviors

While using crystal meth, Matt had unprotected sex with people he didn't know. That type of behavior is common among crystal meth users, and has led to an increase in HIV infection rates. It's one of the many severe consequences of the drug, which also causes mental health problems, brain damage, and even death.

Matt's drug abuse became so bad that he barely graduated high school. Then one night, he came home drunk and stoned after a night out, got into an argument with his parents, and blurted out his secret—that he was gay. They immediately told him to leave. For the next year, his life spiraled downward; he was even homeless for a period of time.

SUBSTANCE ABUSE   47

LGBT young people who have been rejected by their families may end up living on the streets.

"I continued that way for so long, I don't know how I'm still alive," says Matt, who also used cocaine, marijuana, and abused prescription medications. "I should be dead now. And the whole time, I thought it was because I was gay. It was my punishment. That's what they always told me. If you're gay, you're going to use drugs and your life will be ruined. And when that's what happened; I thought they were right."

Sitting in a bar one night, barely conscious, Matt was "probably a few steps away from being dead." He was living with a much older man because he had no place else to go. The man he lived with would buy him food and drugs in exchange for sex.

Self-loathing and depression can lead to dangerous behaviors, creating a destructive downward spiral.

"I felt like my life was worthless, so I didn't care what happened to it," he says. "It was all just about getting more drugs. It didn't matter what I had to do."

Then he met a social worker from a local LGBT community center. She told him about some of the support groups and programs the center offered, and invited him to visit. He did, and it changed his life.

"She saved my life," Matt says. "She helped me get clean. Now I'm in college. I have a boyfriend and a job. I'm really happy. And I'm proud of myself. I have respect for myself now, which I never had before.

"I didn't think I'd be able to have this, because I'm gay. And I think a lot of other gay people think that, too. That's why there's so much drugs and drinking. People don't know it's okay, that they can have something better."

Lesbians and Alcohol Abuse

Excessive alcohol use is far more prevalent among lesbians than it is among heterosexual women. Kara Blake, whose difficulty accepting herself as a lesbian led to overeating and drug abuse, began drinking alcohol when she went to gay bars to meet people.

"It was like that was the only option," she says. "That's what you did on Friday and Saturday nights. You go to the bar. Then it became Sunday, Monday, Tuesday, every day. You'd meet people, but of course they would drink too much, too. So then the relationship would be unhealthy because it was based on something so unhealthy. It was just a crazy cycle that didn't really make any sense. But it's not like you could just go meet a girl at the grocery store and ask her out. At least at a gay bar, you know everyone is gay."

Once Kara got involved in an organization for LGBT students at her college, she began to meet new people and found activities that didn't involve drugs or alcohol. She also participated in campaigns to help teach other people about the dangers of substance abuse.

"I don't think people really understand just how dangerous it is, because it just looks like fun," she says. "But if you look at the statistics, the number of LGBT people who get into serious trouble, you really see that this is something that is destroying our community."

Tobacco Use

The prevalence of tobacco use is much higher among LGBT adults, especially lesbians, than it is in the overall adult population. More than one in four LGBT adults smokes cigarettes, as opposed to one in six straight adults. LGBT teens are four times more likely to smoke than their straight peers.

50　KEEPING PHYSICALLY HEALTHY

Excessive alcohol use is far more prevalent among lesbians than among heterosexual women. Getting drunk is often an attempt to cope with feelings of loneliness and pain.

 Nicotine, the chief chemical in cigarettes, produces feelings of pleasure and reward; and the results are almost instantaneous—nicotine reaches the brain within just ten seconds of inhaling cigarette smoke. This makes cigarettes attractive to people who struggle with the

SUBSTANCE ABUSE 51

Smoking can be a self-destructive behavior and is a major health issue among LGBT people.

social stresses we discussed earlier in the chapter. Yet cigarettes also increase your risk for cancer, heart disease, chronic bronchitis, and other serious diseases. Smoking is one of the leading contributors to poor health among LGBT people.

Finding Options

When people feel they don't belong any place else, they sometimes do what they think they must do to fit in. That was the case for Kara

> **CLOSE-UP: RECOVERY AND REHABILITATION RESOURCES**
>
> There are many structured programs for people who want to break their harmful habits and addictions. Twelve-step recovery programs are based on the successful methods used by Alcoholics Anonymous. People in these programs pass through twelve stages, or steps, toward addiction recovery—beginning by acknowledging the power their addiction has over them and working to replace it with faith in a higher power. There are twelve-step recovery programs for virtually every kind of addiction, including alcohol, cigarettes, heroin and other narcotics, cocaine, sex, food, gambling, and many others.
>
> However, twelve-step programs aren't right for everyone. Fortunately, there are various alternatives, some that are less faith-based and some more so, including SMART Recovery, SOS, and LifeRing. There's also the alternative of inpatient or outpatient rehab, which involves checking into a rehabilitation center for consistent treatment over a number of days, weeks, or even months. There are reputable rehabilitation centers located all across the country.

and Matt, both of whom broke out of dangerous cycles of addiction by participating in 12-step recovery programs.

Increased use of drugs and alcohol is also common among individuals who are HIV positive, particularly gay men. One of the reasons for this is likely the hopelessness some people feel at having an illness that cannot be cured.

Stu, an avid activist for LGBT health issues in San Francisco, began using drugs and alcohol when he was a teenager. Influenced by his parents, who were heavy drinkers, he used drugs and alcohol as a way to

When you like yourself and have caring friends who accept you the way you are, you don't need to abuse drugs or engage in other self-destructive behaviors.

escape the feelings of low self-esteem that resulted from being an overweight kid.

"I tested HIV positive in the late 1980s and felt that I now had permission to drink and do drugs without restriction. I wallowed in self-pity," said Stu, who was also a subject of the 2005 documentary *Do I Look Fat?*

Eventually, he got clean and focused on improving his overall health. He has lived with his illness for decades and now sees that it is not an excuse for abusing drugs and alcohol.

Many resources exist for individuals with substance-abuse issues. In some communities, LGBT organizations offer Alcoholics Anonymous and Narcotics Anonymous meetings specifically for LGBT people. And rehabilitation treatment centers can be found across the country.

The most important thing in steering clear of addiction is education and awareness. Numerous organizations have developed public education campaigns to make people more aware of the dangers of drug and alcohol abuse. Studies have shown that such campaigns have reduced use of crystal meth in the gay community. And peer-based outreach has been even more successful. Within the LGBT community, activists have begun focusing on pride in the community's history to help reduce the shame factor.

"Once I started seeing being gay as just a part of who I am, and I accepted and loved that, I was so much happier," Matt said. "I didn't need drugs, and I didn't need to get drunk. I was happy with myself."

SUBSTANCE ABUSE   55

 TEXT-DEPENDENT QUESTIONS

- What draws people to substances such as alcohol, tobacco, and drugs?
- How does abusing these substances make problems worse instead of better?
- What are some effective ways of confronting substance abuse?

 RESEARCH PROJECTS

- Make a list of activities that might help ease anxiety or stress in a healthier way than relying on drugs or alcohol.
- Make a list of some situations in which you might feel tempted to use substances to feel more at ease.
- If visitors are allowed, sit in on a meeting of a recovery group in your area, and listen to some firsthand stories of dealing with addiction.

SERIES GLOSSARY

Activists: People committed to social change through political and personal action.
Advocacy: The process of supporting the rights of a group of people and speaking out on their behalf.
Alienation: A feeling of separation and distance from other people and from society.
Allies: People who support others in a cause.
Ambiguous: Something unclear or confusing.
Anonymous: Being unknown; having no one know who you are.
Assumption: A conclusion drawn without the benefit of real evidence.
Backlash: An adverse reaction by a large number of people, especially to a social or political development.
Bias: A tendency or preference toward a particular perspective or ideology that interferes with the ability to be impartial, unprejudiced, or objective.
Bigotry: Stubborn and complete intolerance of a religion, appearance, belief, or ethnic background that differs from one's own.
Binary: A system made up of two, and only two, parts.
Bohemian: Used to describe movements, people, or places characterized by nontraditional values and ways of life often coupled with an interest in the arts and political movements.
Caricature: An exaggerated representation of a person.
Celibate: Choosing not to have sex.
Chromosome: A microscopic thread of genes within a cell that carries all the information determining what a person is like, including his or her sex.

Cisgender: Someone who self-identifies with the gender he or she was assigned at birth.

Civil rights: The rights of a citizen to personal and political freedom under the law.

Clichés: Expressions that have become so overused—stereotypes, for example—that they tend to be used without thought.

Closeted: Choosing to conceal one's true sexual orientation or gender identity.

Compensating: Making up for something by trying harder or going further in the opposite direction.

Conservative: Cautious; resistant to change and new ideas.

Controversy: A disagreement, often involving a touchy subject about which differing opinions create tension and strong reactions.

Customs: Ideas and ways of doing things that are commonly understood and shared within a society.

Demonize: Portray something or someone as evil.

Denominations: Large groups of religious congregations united under a common faith and name, and organized under a single legal administration.

Derogatory: Critical or cruel, as in a term used to make a person feel devalued or humiliated.

Deviation: Something abnormal; something that has moved away from the standard.

Dichotomy: Division into two opposite and contradictory groups.

Discrimination: When someone is treated differently because of his or her race, sexual orientation, gender identity, religion, or some other factor.

Disproportionate: A situation where one particular group is overrepresented within a larger group.

Diverse: In the case of a community, one that is made up of people from many different backgrounds.

Effeminate: A word used to refer to men who have so-called feminine qualities.

Emasculated: Having had one's masculinity or manhood taken away.

Empathy: Feeling for another person; putting yourself mentally and emotionally in another person's place.

Empirical evidence: Factual data gathered from direct observation.

Empowering: Providing strength and energy; making someone feel powerful.

Endocrinologist: A medical doctor who specializes in the treatment of hormonal issues.

Epithets: Words or terms used in a derogatory way to put a person down.

The Establishment: The people who hold influence and power in society.

Extremist: Someone who is in favor of using extreme or radical measures, especially in politics and religion.

Flamboyant: Colorful and a bit outrageous.

Fundamentalist: Someone who believes in a particular religion's fundamental principles and follows them rigidly. When the word is used in connection with Christianity, it refers to a member of a form of Protestant Christianity that believes in the strict and literal interpretation of the Bible.

Gay liberation: The movement for the civil and legal rights of gay people that originated in the 1950s and emerged as a potent force for social and political change in the late 1960s and '70s.

Gender: A constructed sexual identity, whether masculine, feminine, or entirely different.

Gender identity: A person's self-image as female, male, or something entirely different, no matter what gender a person was assigned at birth.

Gender roles: Those activities and traits that are considered appropriate to males and females within a given culture.

Gene: A microscopic sequence of DNA located within a chromosome that determines a particular biological characteristic, such as eye color.

Genitalia: The scientific term for the male and female sex organs.

Genocide: The large-scale murder and destruction of a particular group of people.

Grassroots: At a local level; usually used in reference to political action that begins within a community rather than on a national or global scale.

Harassed/harassment: Being teased, bullied, or physically threatened.

Hate crime: An illegal act in which the victim is targeted because of his or her race, religion, sexual orientation, or gender identity.

Homoerotic: Having to do with homosexual, or same-sex, love and desire.

Homophobia: The fear and hatred of homosexuality. A homophobic person is sometimes referred to as a "homophobe."

Horizontal hostility: Negative feeling among people within the same minority group.

Hormones: Chemicals produced by the body that regulate biological functions, including male and female gender traits, such as beard growth and breast development.

Identity: The way a person, or a group of people, defines and understands who they are.

Inborn: Traits, whether visible or not, that are a part of who we are at birth.

Inclusive: Open to all ideas and points of view.

Inhibitions: Feelings of guilt and shame that keep us from doing things we might otherwise want to do.

Internalized: Taken in; for example, when a person believes the negative opinions other people have of him, he has *internalized* their point of view and made it his own.

Interpretation: A particular way of understanding something.

Intervention: An organized effort to help people by changing their attitudes or behavior.

Karma: The force, recognized by both Hindus and Buddhists, that emanates from one's actions in this life; the concept that the good and bad things one does determine where he or she will end up in the next life.

Legitimized: Being taken seriously and having the support of large numbers of people.

LGBT: An initialism that stands for lesbian, gay, bisexual, and transgender. Sometimes a "Q" is added (**LGBTQ**) to include "questioning." "Q" may also stand for "queer."

Liberal: Open to new ideas; progressive; accepting and supportive of the ideas or identity of others.

Liberation: The act of being set free from oppression and persecution.

Mainstream: Accepted, understood, and supported by the majority of people.

Malpractice: When a doctor or other professional gives bad advice or treatment, either out of ignorance or deliberately.

Marginalize: Push someone to the sidelines, away from the rest of the world.

Mentor: Someone who teaches and offers support to another, often younger, person.

Monogamous: Having only one sexual or romantic partner.

Oppress: Keep another person or group of people in an inferior position.

Ostracized: Excluded from the rest of a group.

Out: For an LGBT person, the state of being open with other people about his or her sexual orientation or gender identity.

Outed: Revealed or exposed as LGBT against one's will.

Persona: A character or personality chosen by a person to change the way others perceive them.

Pioneers: People who are the first to try new things and experiment with new ways of life.

Politicized: Aware of one's rights and willing to demand them through political action.

Prejudice: An opinion (usually unfavorable) of a person or a group of people not based on actual knowledge.

Proactive: Taking action taken in advance of an anticipated situation or difficulty.

Progressive: Supporting human freedom and progress.

Psychologists and psychiatrists: Professionals who study the human mind and human behavior. Psychiatrists are medical doctors who can prescribe pills, whereas clinical psychologists provide talk therapy.

Quackery: When an untrained person gives medical advice or treatment, pretending to be a doctor or other medical expert.

The Right: In politics and religion, the side that is generally against social change and new ideas; often used interchangeably with *conservative*.

Segregation: Historically, a system of laws and customs that limited African Americans' access to many businesses, public spaces, schools, and neighborhoods that were "white only."

Sexual orientation: A person's physical and emotional attraction to the opposite sex (heterosexuality), the same sex (homosexuality), both sexes (bisexuality), or neither (asexuality).

Sociologists: People who study the way groups of humans behave.

Spectrum: A wide range of variations.

Stereotype: A caricature; a way to judge someone, probably unfairly, based on opinions you may have about a particular group they belong to.

Stigma: A mark of shame.

Subculture: A smaller group of people with similar interests and lifestyles within a larger group.

Taboo: Something that is forbidden.

Theories: Ideas or explanations based on research, experimentation, and evidence.

Tolerance: Acceptance of, and respect for, other people's differences.

Transgender: People who identify with a gender different from the one they were assigned at birth.

Transphobia: Fear or hatred of transgender people.

Variance: A range of differences within a category such as gender.

Victimized: Subjected to unfair and negative treatment, including violence, bullying, harassment, or prejudice.

FURTHER RESOURCES

The Body: The Complete HIV/AIDS Resource
Index of articles from Gay and Lesbian Medical Association.
www.thebody.com/content/art13665.html

The National Gay and Lesbian Task Force
Advancing full freedom, justice and equality for LGBTQ people.
www.thetaskforce.org

The Trevor Project
The leading national organization providing crisis intervention and suicide prevention services to LGBTQ young people ages 13–24.
www.thetrevorproject.org

Homosexuals Are More Prone to Eating Disorders
Article on the risks for gay men and lesbians.
news.softpedia.com/news/Homosexuals-Are-More-Prone-to-Eating-Disorders-51975.shtml

National Eating Disorders
Supports individuals and families affected by eating disorders, and serves as a catalyst for prevention, cures, and access to quality care.
www.nationaleatingdisorders.org

Avert
Founded in 1986, AVERT has been providing HIV and AIDS information since the start of the epidemic.
www.avert.org

Centers for Disease Control and Prevention
The leading national public health institute of the United States.
www.cdc.gov

12-Step Programs
A nationwide network for treating a full range of addictions.
http://www.12step.org

Secular Organizations for Sobriety (SOS)
A non-spiritual approach to addiction recovery.
http://www.sossobriety.org

SMART Recovery
Self-management for addiction recovery.
http://www.smartrecovery.org

LifeRing Secular Recovery
A secular, abstinence-based, worldwide network of individuals seeking to live *in recovery from addiction.*
http://lifering.org

Gay-friendly Rehab
A list of the best addiction-recovery centers for LBGT patients.
http://www.recovery.org/topics/find-the-best-gay-lesbian-bisexual-transgender-lgbt-addiction-recovery-centers

INDEX

addiction 27, 34, 44–45, 52, 54–55, 63
AIDS 31–34, 41, 45, 62–63
alcohol 14, 26, 42, 44, 49–50, 52–55
Alcoholics Anonymous 52, 54
anorexia nervosa 25

bulimia nervosa 25

condom 16, 33–34, 36–37, 40
crystal meth 44–46, 54

depression 12, 22, 26, 44, 48
discrimination 11–12, 34, 38, 43, 57

eating disorder 14, 20–21, 24–25, 27–29, 62
   anorexia nervosa 25
   bulimia nervosa 25
effeminate 19–20

Gay and Lesbian Medical Association 17, 62
gay bar 20, 45, 49

harassment 31, 38, 42, 58–59
HIV 16, 30–35, 44, 46, 52–53, 63

homophobia 14, 17, 44, 59
   internalized 14, 17
masculinity 18–21, 23, 58
Modern Family 20

National Association of Lesbian and Gay Addiction Professionals 44
National Gay and Lesbian Task Force 16, 62

oppression 12, 60

pregnancy 38–39

rehabilitation centers 28, 52
role models 20, 44

safer sex 16, 31–32, 34–36, 40–41
sexually transmitted disease (STD) 33–37, 41
sexual orientation 13, 22, 27, 32, 39, 58, 61
steroids 24
stereotypes 25, 57, 61
subculture 19, 26, 61
substance abuse 12, 43–54
suicide 9, 12, 16, 62

tobacco 44, 49, 54
Trevor Project 12, 16–17, 62

3162.1
Rod
3/17